Contents

UKULELE

Getting to Know Uke

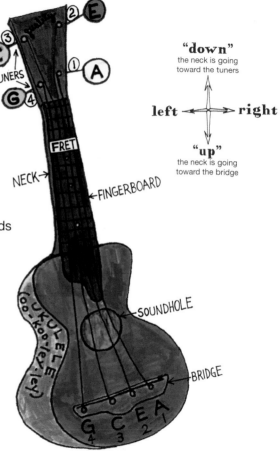

"down"
the neck is going
toward the tuners

left ← → right

"up"
the neck is going
toward the bridge

Portuguese sailors brought the ukulele with them to Hawaii
in the 19th century. The beauty of the uke is its versatility. The
four basic models are soprano, concert, tenor and baritone. The chords
in this book are for soprano, concert and tenor ukuleles tuned
to G C E A.

Pictured here are the parts of the ukulele that we will refer
to as we show you how to play.

Take your ukulele in your hands. Hold the neck of the ukulele
in your left hand in the curve between your thumb and first finger.
Hold the body of the uke against your chest
with your right forearm, snug as a bug.

FLIP FLAP

TUNING by EAR

Using an A 440 tuning fork
Strike it on your knee and hold the stem of the
fork against your ear or on the top of your instrument.

You should hear a good, clear "A" note. Hum along with the note.
Pluck string #1, the "A" string on the uke. Using the tuning peg for
that string, turn it up or down a little at a time to make the
note higher or lower to match the "A" sound.

**Once you have "A" sounding good, tune
the rest of the strings like this:**

1. Fret the 2nd String (E) on the 5th Fret to match the sound with the
   open 1st String (A.)
2. Fret the 3rd String (C) on the 4th Fret to match the sound with the open
   2nd String (E.)
3. Put your left finger on the 4th String (G) just behind the 5th Fret
   and match the sound of the open 3rd String (C.)

Voila!

The NUMBER SYSTEM
Find your favorite Key

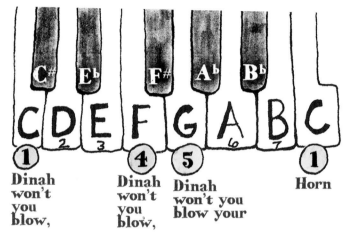

① Dinah won't you blow,

④ Dinah won't you blow,

⑤ Dinah won't you blow your

① Horn

Uke chords:

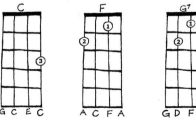

The number system is a simple way to communicate the chords to play, whether the musician can read music or not. A chord is a group of (typically 3 or more) notes sounded together to accompany the melody of the song. Here's how the number system works in this book. Most Ukalalien® songs are simple 3-chord folk songs.

Let's begin by looking at the notes in the "C major scale": C-D-E-F-G-A-B-C. Now, let's give each of those notes a number: C=1, D=2, E=3, etc. In the "Number System", the number assigned to a note, corresponds with the number assigned to the chord used in a song. So, if the chords used in the song to the left are: C-F-G^7, they can also be referred as the "1-4-5" chords in the "key of C". If we want to play the same song in the "key of G" and the "G major scale" is: G-A-B-C-D-E-F#-G, then our "1-4-5" chords are "G-C-D".

C	D	E	F	G	A	B	C
1	**2**	**3**	**4**	**5**	**6**	**7**	**8**
DO	RE	MI	FA	SO	LA	TI	DO

The Chord Group charts (left and right FLIP FLAPS) above the pages of your *Ukalaliens® Songbook* give you six Keys to play the songs in. The Keys listed under the song titles in this book are the Keys you will use in the Chord Group chart. We will play in one Key on the recording for you to play and sing along with. Then you can try out different Keys to sing the songs in to discover the Key you like best for your voice. There are more chord groups but these six will give you a place to begin.

There is a Chord Glossary on the bottom of the back FLIP FLAP. Find other chords that may not be listed in the Chord Groups above. Have fun!

There are 8-notes in a "diatonic scale" (do-re-mi....) In the Key of C, these notes are C-D-E-F-G-A-B-C. Notes in any Key can also be referred to as "do-re-mi-fa-so-la-ti-do" and "1-2-3-4-5-6-7-8."

The Key of C is based on the C scale, the only scale with no flats or sharps (no black keys.)

When you count 1 - 4 - 5 in any other Keys, use the notes that fit (sound right) in the 8-note scale. To see the 1-4-5 in some other keys, look at the Chord Groups on the FLIP FLAPS on pages 2 & 37.
(Example: Key of C = C-F-G. Key of D = D-G-A.)

Singers sing best where their voices are comfortable. If the Key is too low to sing in, we simply move the Key up to a higher note and make that the "1" and count from there.

To find the easiest place to sing, start in C. If your voice is struggling, move your voice up or down to a different Key and chord group until you find the one you like the best. The chord that matches the "1" in your song is your new Key. Use the chord group for that key for a 1-4-5 song. The FLIP FLAPS Chord Groups are a simple starting place. There are more chords and keys to explore from here!

LEFT HAND TECHNIQUE
Chording, Hammer-On, Pull-Off, Slap & Slide

Some techniques, tricks of the trade & cheap theatrics! Fretting (pressing down on a string) the neck with the fingers of your left hand to make chords is one of the first things to learn.

The "C" chord is easy!

To begin, curl your left hand and press the tip of your left ring finger (3) onto the first string at the 3rd fret. With your right hand first finger, gently strum your fingernail across all the strings—4, 3, 2, 1. You are playing the C chord!

Strum down, down, down, down. Try to play a full, clean sounding chord. If the strings are buzzing, fret a little harder. If they sound sharp, fret a little lighter. Keep your touch flexible enough to make a good clean sound.

Special Effects

A "**hammer-on**" (as coined by Pete Seeger) is created when the player plucks the string and, while the note is still ringing, quickly frets the vibrating string. A "hammer-on" on the "C" chord occurs when you pluck the open "A" string and quickly fret it at the 3rd fret.

A "**pull-off**" is the opposite of a "hammer-on." A "pull-off 'on the C chord will occur when you pluck the A string (fretted at the 3rd fret) and then quickly pull your finger off the 3rd fret. The note will descend from C to A.

A "**slap**" occurs when you strum a chord and let your palm land on the strings, quickly muting the strings at the tail end of the downward stroke.

A "**slide**" occurs when you fret below where you would normally fret on the fingerboard and quickly "slide" up the fingerboard to where you would normally fret that chord or string. Example: Play a G chord shape on the 1st and 2nd fret (instead of the 2nd and 3rd fret.) Strum it and "slide" up to the 2nd and 3rd fret while the strings are ringing. One strum, two notes!

tip:
To develop strength chording with your left hand, FLEX!

Press to play the chord and release lightly in between strums and chord changes to flex your hand "on" (to play the chord) and "off" (in between strums and chord changes.) Keep your fingers as close to the strings as you can, ready to play with both hands.

RIGHT HAND STRUMS

Hold the uke neck in your left hand (in the curve between your thumb and first finger.) Curl your Ring Finger (3) on the left hand and with your fingertip press the first string at the third fret to make a C chord. Holding the uke in position, as you're strumming up and down, make sure your wrist is nice and loose.

Downstroke: Curl the fingers on your right hand and opening your hand in a downward motion lightly brush across all the strings with the fingernail of your Index Finger (1) or Thumb (T.)

Upstroke: Return from the downstroke with a gentle upswing brushing the strings on the way back with the pad of your first finger.

1	2	3	4	&

Strum 1: Down, Down, Down, Down, Up

↓   ↓   ↓   ↓   ↑

The Upstroke (&) is a 1/2 beat and takes half the time of the downstroke.

1	2	&	3	4	&

Strum 2: DOWN, Down, Up, DOWN, Down, Up

↓   ↓   ↑   ↓   ↓   ↑

1	2	3	&	1	2	3	&

Strum 3: DOWN, Down, Down, and DOWN, Down, Down, and

Waltz   ↓   ↓   ↓   ↑   ↓   ↓   ↓   ↑

Curl the fingers on your right hand and lightly brush across the strings with the fingernail of your Index Finger (1) or Thumb (T.) When you get used to strumming, try your hand at making up strums with combinations of upstrokes and downstrokes just for fun. Once your right wrist gets comfortable you will find your strums following the swing of the song with a natural feel and expression all your own.

9

RIGHT HAND

Simple Picking Patterns

In this fingerpicking method set your right hand with the tip of your ring finger or pinky anchored on the top below the soundhole so your hand is in place as your Thumb, Index & Middle fingers pick.

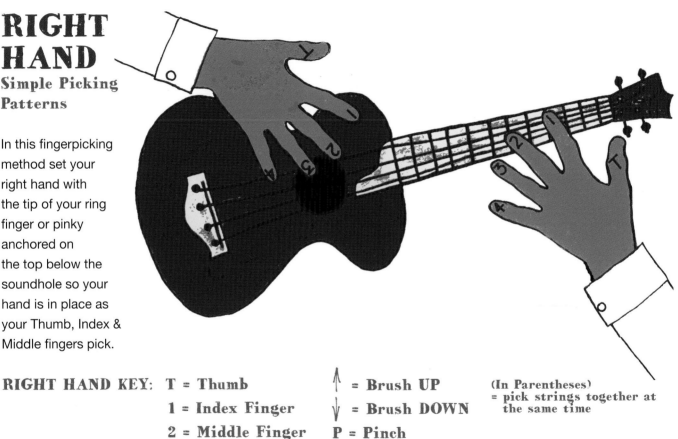

RIGHT HAND KEY:　　T = Thumb　　↑ = Brush UP　　(In Parentheses)
　　　　　　　　　　　1 = Index Finger　↓ = Brush DOWN　= pick strings together at
　　　　　　　　　　　2 = Middle Finger　P = Pinch　　　the same time

To fingerpick, play the pattern over and over until it becomes a rolling pattern of notes that fit the rhythm of the song. Once you have the basics, make up new patterns of your own. When you're ready, add one new thing — a brush, two-string pinch, hammer-on, pull off, slide here and there, up and down. See how you can play, strum and pick what you've learned in new ways (your ways!) Keep the beat, tap your feet. Start slowly and build up to a comfortable steady pace. Play to the music the way you feel it. Enjoy exploring!

Pick 1 4/4

Pluck This String:	4/G	2/E	3/C	1/A
With This Finger:	**T**	**1**	**T**	**2**

Thumb – Index – Thumb – Middle

Pick 2 4/4

Pluck This String:	4/G	2/E	3/C	1/A	4/G	2/C	Brush DOWN & UP
With This Finger:	**T**	**1**	**T**	**2**	**T**	**1**	↓ ↑

Thumb – Index – Thumb – Middle – Thumb – Index – Brush Down & Up

Pinch 1 4/4

Pluck This String:	4/G	(3/C	2/E)		4/G	(3/C	2/E)
With This Finger:	**T**	(**T**	**1**)		**T**	(**T**	**1**)

Thumb (Thumb-Index)   Thumb (Thumb-Index)

Pinch 2 Waltz 3/4

Pluck This String:	4/G	(3/C	2/E	1/A)	(3/C	2/E	1/A)
With This Finger:	**T**	(**T**	**1**	**2**)	(**T**	**1**	**2**)

Thumb (Thumb – Index – Middle)   (Thumb – Index – Middle)

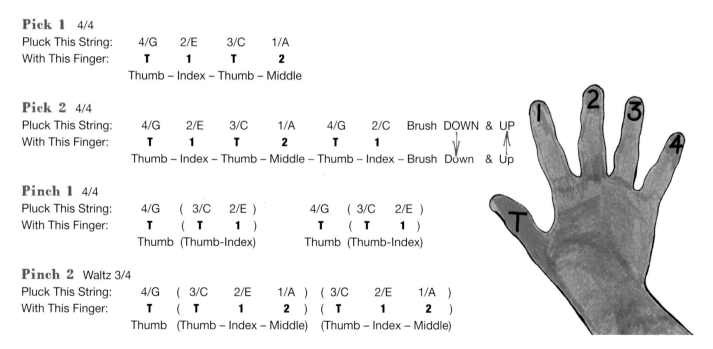

THE SONGS

Listen to the Ukalaliens® CD and Follow the Songs! (Enclosed inside back cover.)

The songs are arranged in alphabetical order in the book. The songs on the Ukalaliens® CD are in order of EASE. Follow the CD and you will find it easy to play and sing along with the songs. Some are old songs we grew up with in the kitchen and singing around the campfire. Some are new songs we made up and are fun to play and sing on the uke.

To get started, we invite you to listen to all of the songs. Be brave! Tune up and play along. Don't be intimidated if your dog begins to howl and leaves the room. Hear how the song goes and then sing and play along on your ukulele. With what you learn by following the songs here in the Ukalaliens® Songbook, you can begin to play familiar favorites or even make up some of your own songs.

We recorded the songs in Keys that work for us. If the Key we sing it in is too high or too low for your voice, play with us as long as it takes to learn the song and then change it to a Key and the chord group that works better for you. **The numbers in the songbook will work in any Key.** The numbers are placed over the word where the chord should be played in the song. You can take every song here and play it in all six Keys on the Flip Flaps used in this book and hear what it sounds like. Then play and sing the song in the Key that fits your voice.

ANNABELLE

Steve Einhorn ©1998/BMI ℗ Katidoo

TRACK 9 / Key of G

5   1   4   5   1

Annabelle, won't you come back home, there's supper on the stove

5   1   4   5   1

You've been away such a long, long time, I hardly know you

CHORUS

1   4 5   4 1

Won't you come back home, there's supper on the stove

1   4 5   4 1

Won't you come back home, there's supper on the stove

Precious children grow so fast then they leave us all alone

We've got to love them while we can, before we're dead and gone

RELEASE

5   1   4

Ooh - ooh - ooh - ooh - ooh,

5   1

ooh - ooh - ooh - ooh   (2x)

13

BOLD FISHERMAN

TRAD/Arr.©2003/BMI℗ Katidoo

TRACK 10 / Key of C
WALTZ 3/4 TEMPO

1   **5**
There was a bold fisherman
                    1
who sailed out to Pimlico
1   **4**   **5**   **1**
To slew the wily codfish & the bold mackerel
1   **4**
When he got to Pimlico
     4   **1**
The stormy winds began to blow,
     6m   **4**
& His little boat went wibble-wobble
  5   **1**
& overboard went he

CHORUS

          1   **5**
Singing twinkle doodle dum, twinkle doodle dum
1   **5**
'Twas the highly interesting song he sung,
1   **5**
Twinkle doodle dum, twinkle   doodle   dum
5   **1 5**   **1 5** + **1 5 1 5**
Sang the Bold Fisherman.

He wriggled and he scriggled in the ocean so briny-o
He yellowed and he bellowed for help but in vain
Downward he did gently glide to the bottom of the silvery tide but
previously to this he cried,
"Fare thee well, Mary Jane!"

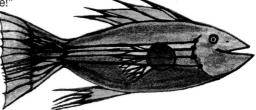

His ghost walked at midnight by the bed of his Mary Jane
When he told her how dead he was, she said, "I'll go mad"
"If my lovey is so dead", said she,
"No joy on earth there'll ever be,
I never more will happy be" and she went raving mad.

CARELESS LOVE
TRADITIONAL

TRACK 11 / Key of F

1   **5**   **1**
Love, oh love, oh careless love
1   **5**
Love, oh love, oh careless love
1   **4**
Love, oh love, oh careless love,
1   **5**   **1**
Oh see what careless love has done

I cried last night and the night before
I cried last night and the night before
Oh I cried last night and the night before
Going to cry tonight and cry no more

CRAWDAD HOLE
TRADITIONAL

1
You get a line an' I'll get a pole, honey,
1   **5**
You'll get a line an' I'll get a pole, babe,
1
You'll get a line an' I'll get a pole,
4
We're goin' down the crawdad hole,
1   **5**   **1**
Honey, baby, mine

What you gonna do when the pond goes dry, honey,
What you gonna do when the pond goes dry, baby,
What you gonna do when the pond goes dry,
Stand on the bank watch the crawdads die,
Honey, baby, mine.

Yonder come a man with a sack on his back, honey,
Yonder come a man with a sack on his back, babe,
Yonder come a man with a sack on his back,
Crawdads crawlin' back to back.
Honey, baby, mine.

16

EL BELLE

Steve Einhorn
©1998/BMI ℗ Katidoo

TRACKS 13 + 14 / Key of C

*...Steve's melody for his sister, Ellen.
A little melody to play over and over, to
explore one little tune 100 ways...*

```
C  Dm   C   Dm   C
// ////  ////  ////  //
1  2m   1   2m   1
```

*Play these songs over and over. Repetition is the key
to mastering the mechanics of changing from one chord
to another. While playing the songs experiment with
the pull-off, hammer-on, slap and slide.*

MINOR RIFF

Steve Einhorn
©2007/BMI ℗ Katidoo

TRACK 15 / Key of Dm

...a roll with minor chords

```
4m    1m    5    1m
Gm    Dm    A    Dm
////  ////  ////  ////
```

```
4m    1m    5    1m
Gm    Dm    A    Dm
////  ////  ////  ////
```

GUABI, GUABI

TRAD/Arr. ©2003/BMI ℗ Katidoo

TRACK 16 / Key of F

A phonetic way to sing this Zulu folk song from the Nde-Ele tribe.

1   **4**   **1**

Guabi, Guabi cooz wan lay tom byami

5   **1**

Ee-so-lay gambay shoe-ee ahn tan-na

1   **4**   **1**

Guabi, Guabi cooz wan lay tom byami

1   **5**   **1**

Ee-so-lay gambay shoe-ee ahn tan-na

1   **4**   **1**

N'yay zon tengee la ma banza

1   **5**   **1**

Easy weetchie lay banana

1   **4**   **1**

N'yay zon tengee la ma banza

1   **5**   **1**

Easy weetchie lay banana

The original words are a mix of Zulu & French:

Guabi, Guabi, guzwangle notamb yami
(Hear, Guabi, Guabi, I have a girlfriend)

Ihlale nkamben', shu'ngyamtanda
(She lives at Nkamben, sure I love her)

Ngizamtenge la mabanzi, iziwichi le banana."
(I will buy her buns, sweets, and bananas.)

HOME ON THE RANGE
TRADITIONAL

TRACK 17 / Key of C

1   **4**
Oh, give me a home where the buffalo roam
       1   **5**
Where the deer and the antelope play
      1   **4**
Where seldom is heard a discouraging word
      1   **5**   **1**
And the skies are not cloudy all day

How often at night where the heavens are bright
With the light of the glittering stars
Have I stood there amazed and asked as I gazed
If their glory exceeds that of ours

CHORUS

1   **5**   **1**
Home, home on the range
       1   **5**
Where the deer and the antelope play
      1   **4**
Where seldom is heard a discouraging word
      1   **5**   **1**
And the skies are not cloudy all day

Where the air is so pure, the zephyrs so free
The breezes so balmy and light
That I would not exchange my home on the range
                    For all of the cities so bright

I'VE BEEN WORKING ON THE RAILROAD

TRADITIONAL

TRACK 18 / Key of G

1
I've been working on the railroad

4   **1**
All the livelong day

1
I've been working on the railroad

5
Just to pass the time away

5   **1**
Can't you hear the whistle blowing

4   **1**
Rise up so early in the morn

4   **1**
Can't you hear the captain shouting

1   **5**   **1**
Dinah, blow your horn!

1   **4**
Dinah, won't you blow, Dinah, won't you blow

5   **1**
Dinah, won't you blow your horn

1   **4**
Dinah, won't you blow, Dinah, won't you blow

5   **1**
Dinah, won't you blow your horn

1
Someone's in the kitchen with Dinah

1   **5**
Someone's in the kitchen I know

1   **4**
Someone's in the kitchen with Dinah

5   **1**
Strumming on the old banjo, and singing

1   **5**
Fee, fi, fiddly i o, Fee, fi, fiddly i o

1   **4**   **5**   **1**
Fee, fi, fiddly i o, Strumming on the old banjo!

MICHAEL ROW THE BOAT ASHORE
TRADITIONAL

Go to the qualityfolk.com Ukalaliens page online to listen, play along and download MP3 Key of C

1   **4 1**
Michael row the boat ashore, hallelujah
1   **4**   **5 1**
Michael row the boat ashore, hallelujah

Sister help to trim the sails, hallelujah
Sister help to trim the sails, hallelujah

Jordan river is deep and wide, hallelujah
Got a home on the other side, hallelujah

OLD BULLFROG

Kate Power ©2003/BMI ℗ Katidoo

TRACK 19
Key of C

1　　**4**
Old bullfrog, sitting by the river
1　　　　**5**
Lizard on a log, whatcha gonna give her
1　　　　**4**
Flies all around, grab a few for dinner
5　　　　**1**　　**5**　　**1**
Polywogs swimming along-o, long- o, long-o
4　**1**　**5**　**1**

CHORUS

1　　**4**　**1**　　**5**　**1**　　**4**　**5**　**1**
Old bullfrog,　　Old bullfrog,　　Old bullfrog

Bees in a hive, makin' up some honey
Turtle takes a dive, sure do look funny
Never need to try to make a little money
Livin' in the heart o'little Eden, Eden, Eden

Sip a'clear water, easy on yer liver
Watch a lilypod or a hummingbird a quiver
Sweet afternoon on the sunny Sandy River
Salmon do a dosy-doe, dosy-doe, dosy-doe

23

OLD JOE CLARK

TRADITIONAL

TRACK 20
Use the Key of F chord group
(this is in the Key of C)

5

Old Joe Clark, the preacher's son

4

Preached all over the plain

5

The only text he ever knew

5   **4**   **5**

Was High Low Jack and the game

Old Joe Clark had a mule
His name was Morgan Brown
And every tooth in that mule's head
Was sixteen inches round

CHORUS

5

Fare thee well Old Joe Clark

4

Fare thee well I say

5

Fare thee well Old Joe Clark

5   **4**   **5**

I'm a-goin' away

Old Joe Clark had a house
Fifteen stories high
And every story in that house
Was filled with chicken pie

I went down to Old Joe's house
He invited me to supper
I stumped my toe on the table leg
And stuck my nose in the butter

PRETTY LITTLE GIRL (for Lucy)

Kate Power ©2008/BMI ℗ Katidoo

TRACK 21 / Key of A

CHORUS

1

Where did you go, my pretty little girl?

5   **1**

I've been up on the mountain, been around the world

1

You turned my heart, sand into a pearl

5   **1**

Little girl, where did you go?

I was knocking on your door, there was nobody home
I knocked and I knocked my knuckle to the bone
Then I went next door, called you on the telephone
Little girl, where did you go?

Back in the beginning I took you for a ride
To the top of the mountain and down the other side
Then my heart stowed away, I took to the tide
    Little girl, where did you go?

I was tossing on the ocean, rolling on the sea
Till I landed on the shore of a foreign country
I couldn't speak a word to anybody
Little girl, where did you go?

I don't need a knick-knack, no money, no gold,
No tempest in a teapot or a faery tale told
One sweet little kiss before I'm too old
Little girl, where did you go?

SHADY GROVE
TRADITIONAL

TRACK 22
Use the Key of C chord group (this is in the Key of Am)

6m   **5**   **6m**   **6m**
Shady Grove, my little love, Shady Grove, my dear
1   **5**   **6m**   **5**   **6m**
Shady Grove, my little love, I'm going to leave you here

Cheeks as red as a blooming rose
And eyes of the deepest brown
You are the darling of my heart
Stay till the sun goes down

I wish I had a big grey horse
And corn to feed him on
Pretty little girl to stay at home
And feed him when I'm gone

Went to see my Shady Grove
She was standing in the door
Shoes and stockings in her hands
Her little bare feet on the floor

A kiss from pretty little Shady Grove
Is sweet as brandy wine
There's no little girl in this old world
That's prettier than mine!

STUDY WAR NO MORE

TRADITIONAL

TRACK 23 / Key of C

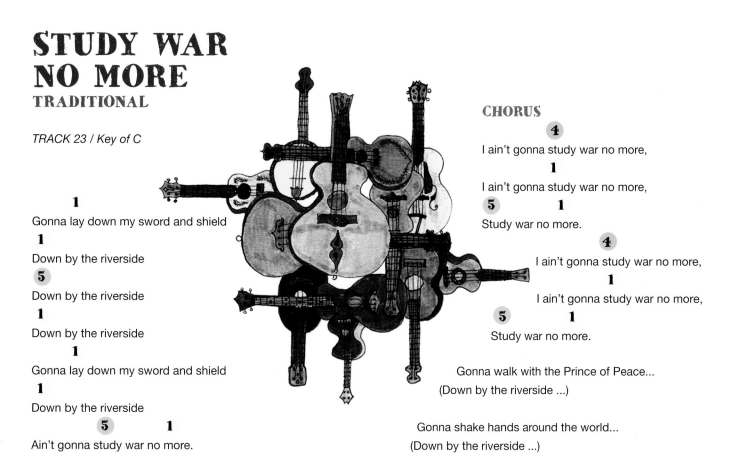

1

Gonna lay down my sword and shield

1

Down by the riverside

5

Down by the riverside

1

Down by the riverside

1

Gonna lay down my sword and shield

1

Down by the riverside

5   **1**

Ain't gonna study war no more.

CHORUS

4

I ain't gonna study war no more,

1

I ain't gonna study war no more,

5   **1**

Study war no more.

4

I ain't gonna study war no more,

1

I ain't gonna study war no more,

5   **1**

Study war no more.

Gonna walk with the Prince of Peace...

(Down by the riverside ...)

Gonna shake hands around the world...

(Down by the riverside ...)

SWING LOW, SWEET CHARIOT
TRADITIONAL

*Go to the qualityfolk.com
Ukalaliens page online to listen,
play along and download
MP3 Key of C*

1   **4** **1**
Swing low, sweet chariot
1   **5**
Coming for to carry me home
1   **4** **1**
Swing low, sweet chariot
1   **5**   **1**
Coming for to carry me home

I looked over Jordan and what did I see
Coming for to carry me home
A band of angels coming after me
Coming for to carry me home

I'm sometimes up and I'm sometimes down
Coming for to carry...
But still my soul is heavenly bound
Coming for to carry...

If I get there before you do
Coming for to carry...
I'll cut a hole and pull you through
Coming for to carry...

If you get there before I do
Coming for to carry...
Tell all my friends I'm coming too
Coming for to carry...

THE FOX
TRADITIONAL

TRACK 24 / Key of C

1
The Fox went out on a chilly night
5
He prayed for the moon to give him light
1   **4**
He had many a mile to go that night
1   **5**   **1**
Before he reached the town-o,
5   **1**
town-o, town-o
4   **1**
He had many a mile to go that night
5   **1**
Before he reached the town-o

He ran till he came to the farmers pen
The ducks and the geese were kept therein
He said a couple of you are gonna grease my chin
Before I leave this town-o,
town-o, town-o
A couple of you are gonna grease my chin
Before I leave this town-o

He grabbed the great goose by the neck
He threw a duck across his back
And he didn't mind the quack, quack, quack
And the legs all danglin'
down-o, down-o, down-o
He didn't mind the quack, quack, quack
and the legs all danglin' down-o

Well the old gray Woman jumped out of bed
Out of the window she popped her head
Cryin' John, John, the great goose is gone
The Fox is on the town-o, town-o, town-o
John, John the great goose is gone
And the Fox is on the town-o

29

THE MORE WE GET TOGETHER
TRADITIONAL

TRACK 25 / Key of C

1

The more we get together

5 **1**

Together, together

1

The more we get together

5 **1**

The happier we'll be.

5 **1**

For your friends are my friends

5 **1**

And my friends are your friends,

1

The more we get together

5

The happier we'll be.

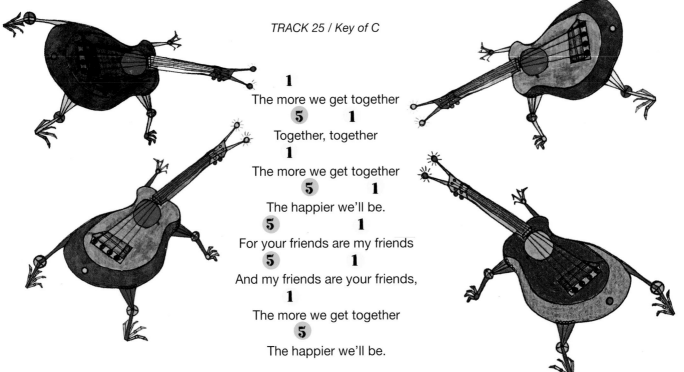

THESE ARE MY MOUNTAINS

TRAD/Arr ©2005 Kate Power & Steve Einhorn/BMI℗Katidoo

TRACK 26 / Key of A

5   **1**   **4**
For fame and for fortune I wandered the earth
       1   **5**
But now I return to the land of my birth
              1   **4**
I brought back my treasures but only to find
       1   **5**   **1** **4** **1**
They're less than the pleasures I first left behind

CHORUS (same as verses)
For these are my mountains, this is my glen
The days of my childhood, I'll see them again
No land will ever tempt me, nor far will I roam
For these are my mountains
& I'm going home

Just been by the road sign and I'm going back
The lark overhead wings a welcoming cry
No longer the droll plight; once more I will see
Sure, it's there that my heart lies, there I would be

Kind faces will meet me and welcome me in
And oh, how they'll greet me back home again
This night 'round the fireside, sad songs will be sung
At last I'll be speaking in my old mother tongue

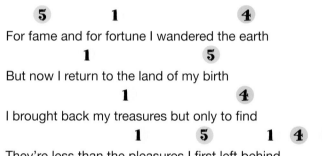

UKULELE BLUES

Steve Einhorn

©2009/BMI ℗ Katidoo

TRACK 27 / Key of A

1
When I'm feeling lonely
1
Nobody hangin' round
1
Nothin' else can cheer me up
1
'Cept that sweet ukulele sound
4
I really love my baby
1
I'll tell you the reason why
5
When she plays her ukulele
4   **1**
It's like an angel singin' in the sky

You may say I'm crazy
Or you may think I'm cool
But one thing I can tell you
I ain't nobody's fool
Take a look around you
Tell me what you see
It seems like everybody I know
Got that ukulele insanity

I got my ukulele
I'm gonna play it all over town
Gonna play it in the mornin'
Play it till that evenin' sun go down
Ukes in my kitchen
Ukes in the hall
I got ukes in the basement
I'm hearing the ukulele call

(Kate's verse)
People stop your fighting
Trade your guns and all your war
For a little ukulele
Find that peace you're looking for
Watch a total stranger
Turn into a friend
No worries, there's no danger
It's a Ukalalien!

UNDER THE MOON

Kate Power ©2008/BMI ℗ Katidoo

Track 28 / Key of C - Strummed
Track 29 - Picked
Track 30 - Picked & Strummed

1   **4**   **1**   **5**
One single bicycle under the moon
1   **4**   **1**   **5**
Circling wheels turning home
1   **4**   **1**   **5**
Road after road, you'll be getting there soon
1   **4**   **1** **5**
With memories full of your roaming!

CHORUS

1   **4**
And here's to another day's ride
1   **5**
Good road up and down the next hill
1
Good neighbors to greet you
4
And old friends to meet you
1   **5**   **1** **4**
To welcome you in from the ride
1   **5**   **1** **5** **1**
To welcome you in from the ride

Turn after turn you can follow the road
Searching your own heart's desire
Riding today in your own rodeo
Then come settle in by the fire

Two thousand bicycles under the moon
Circling wheels turning home
Road after road, we'll be getting there soon
With memories full of our roaming!

UNDER THE MOON
pinch tab

Key of C

This song is "pinched" with thumb and first finger on the right hand throughout the song. Kate plays it by pinching the designated strings shown here with her thumb and first finger together at the same time, one syllable at a time. Follow the chart for a visual map. Listen to the recording to hear how it sounds and follow along. If there's a rest between notes, just pick the open 4th string in time to the moments of rest between words.

tip:
x = pick this string but don't fret it
● = pick & fret here

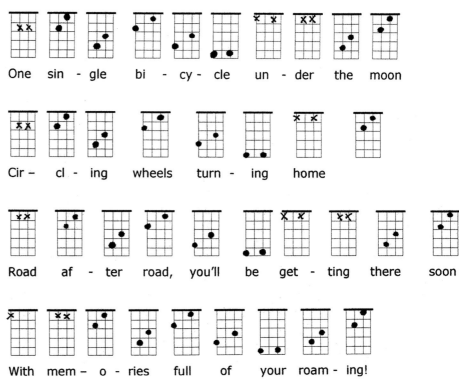

One   sin – gle   bi – cy – cle   un – der   the   moon

Cir – cl – ing   wheels   turn – ing   home

Road   af – ter   road,   you'll   be   get – ting   there   soon

With   mem – o – ries   full   of   your   roam – ing!

34

CHORUS

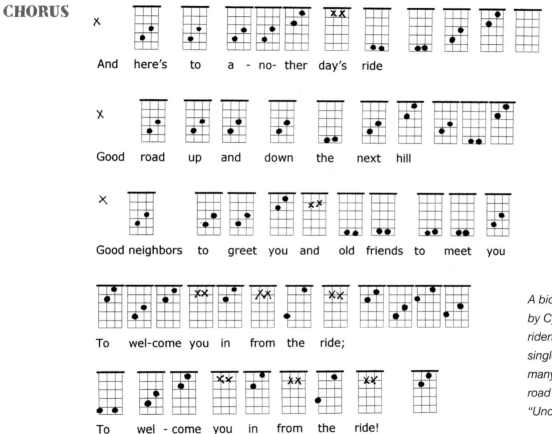

And   here's   to   a - no- ther   day's   ride

Good   road   up   and   down   the   next   hill

Good neighbors   to   greet   you   and   old   friends   to   meet   you

To   wel-come   you   in   from   the   ride;

To   wel - come   you   in   from   the   ride!

A bicycle lullaby inspired by Cycle Oregon and 2000 riders ready to roll as one single bicycle joins with many for a good ride, good road and a better world, "Under the Moon."

Discover the Joy of the Ukulele!

Join the Ukalaliens® movement! Make beautiful music with everybody!

It's a vast and wondrous world. With the *Ukalaliens® Songbook* you will learn to play ukulele and sing along. Let this wonderful little instrument open the gates to your musical life.

Start your own Ukalaliens® group and gather with friends and neighbors to play music and sing songs!

Join our email list at www.qualityfolk.com for news, more information, music, art, books and handy guides from Quality Folk.

Contact us at folks@qualityfolk.com.

Quality Folk is dedicated to ukes without borders and harmonizing community all over the world.

"Have Ukes Will Travel"

TRACK LIST

1. Introduction
2. Getting to Know Uke
3. Tuning by Ear
4. C, F & G Chords
5. The Number system
6. Strums
7. Special Effects
8. Fingerpicking
9. Annabelle
10. Bold Fisherman
11. Careless Love
12. Crawdad Hole
13. El Belle
    Picking & Strumming
    Apart
14. El Belle
    Pick & Strum Together
15. Minor Riff
16. Guabi, Guabi
17. Home on the Range

18. I've Been Working
    on the Railroad
19. Old Bullfrog
20. Old Joe Clark
21. Pretty LIttle Girl (for Lucy)
22. Shady Grove
23. Study War No More
24. The Fox
25. The More We Get Together
26. These Are My Mountains
27. Ukulele Blues
28. Under the Moon - Strummed
29. Under the Moon - Picked
30. Under the Moon
    - Picked & Strummed
31. Closing

FLIP FLAP

NOTE

The songs "Michael Row the Boat Ashore" on page 22 and "Swing Low, Sweet Chariot" on page 28 were not recorded on the CD. You can download MP3 files of these songs for free at www.qualityfolk.com on the Ukalaliens page online.

THE FOLLOWING SONGS

used in this book are on recordings by Kate Power & Steve Einhorn and are available by visiting www.qualityfolk.com:

Annabelle - "Harbour", "Pearls: The Tribute
    Collection", "Winterfolk XV (live)"

Bold Fisherman - "Tales from Puddletown"

El Belle - "Harbour", "Brick & Mortar"

Guabi, Guabi - "Tales from Puddletown",
    "Brick & Mortar"

Old Bullfrog - "Tales from Puddletown"

Pretty Little Girl (for Lucy) - "Brick & Mortar"

These Are My Mountains - "Now & Then"

Under the Moon - "Brick & Mortar",
    "Bicycle Songs"

About the CD ▸

From tuning your ukulele to playing the songs,
the CD will help you learn to chord,
strum, pick and sing along.

Once you play the songs in the keys recorded here, explore singing
them in other Keys using the Chord Group charts on the FLIP FLAPS.
You can adapt what you learn here in the *Ukalaliens® Songbook*
to play with all kinds of songs. There are countless ways to play
the ukulele and there's always room for one more.

Happy playing!

— Steve & Kate